River and Mountains,
Amy K. Epstein

AFLOAT

AFLOAT

JOHN REIBETANZ

Brick Books

Library and Archives Canada Cataloguing in Publication

Reibetanz, John
    Afloat / John Reibetanz.

Poems.
ISBN 978-1-926829-82-1

    I. Title.

PS8585.E448A35 2013   C811'.54   C2013-900060-7

We acknowledge the Canada Council for the Arts, the Government of Canada through the Canada Book Fund, and the Ontario Arts Council for their support of our publishing program.

The author photo was taken by Timothy Reibetanz.

This book is set in Minion Pro, designed by Robert Slimbach and released in 1990 by Adobe Systems.

The cover image is a detail from "River and Mountains" by Amy K. Epstein.

Design and layout by Cheryl Dipede.
Printed and bound by Sunville Printco Inc.

Brick Books
431 Boler Road, Box 20081
London, Ontario N6K 4G6
www.brickbooks.ca

To Julie,

the song's source

CONTENTS

III

AIRBORNE

I

WATERBORNE

—

THE LOVE OF WATER

All nature, from the crag windbreakered in granite
that melts into the nuzzling of the clouds' wet snouts,

to the motes of grit that rise up every morning
and dance in a fountain over the windowsill,

all nature wants to be water. Curled tongues of fire
and sharp tongues of wind stutter and lisp through forests,

longing for the fluency of streams. Clays trapped in
marble fifty million years ago still practice

ripple and purl in rehearsal for the aeon
that will free their liquid hearts, Virginia creeper

clambers on splay-fingered hands up walls and treetrunks
to throw itself down in cascading sprays, even

heaven seeks out lakes where its unfrozen double
pulses. Still more besotted, water dotes on the rest

of nature. Rain, the sky's gift of spirit, so pure
a distillate of blue it abstains from colour,

falls all over the earth, and snowflakes leave unique
designs they've spun their lives into, coming undone

to kiss the same ground the river's whitest water,
charging seaward, turns inside out to wave back at.

Starving for love, the pilgrim waterdrop shivers
under its hood of light, dwindles to mist, and slips

into crevasses between crumbs of soil, to rise
as breath through root hairs and be at one with the trees.

Or with you, for water also loves the nature
that is human. Kissing lips, then tongue, it races

down throat-rapids, threads through bone into your very
marrow and, in a blush of passion, spills over

and floods the heart's chambers scarlet. Your smitten heart
loves back, a lifetime of embraces fluttering

like eyelids when they caress the film of water
pressing against your lenses. You look through them at

a dead tree leaning across a stream. The bleached trunk
so yearns to become water, it has given up

branches and bark in working its way from cedar
to drift. Now pain puts on a coat of warm water

and runs down your cheek. Like the ocean that loved all
nature into first life, it kisses you with salt.

INTO RIVERS

From the German of Paul Celan

Into rivers north of the future

I cast the net that you

tentatively weight

with stonescribbled shadows.

FLOATER

   Too slight to nudge the needle
on a seismograph, a tremor swept
   the globe of my eye last night.

   Now every place the eyelid
lifts its shade, the same shred of wreckage
   washes up on the landscape.

   No more still life: over pears
glazed centuries ago on canvas
   a fly in my eye grazes.

   A phantom inkspot lands in
between inspiration and my hand
   and tracks the clean white paper.

   Broken away, a dark new
moon in erratic orbit, it draws
   an ocean of doubts towards it

   about the mother planet.
How stable is the old high roller?
   How supportive? Taking in

   the sights, we fix our tripod
on a bubble, *terra* no firmer
   than filmy air. Earth's shifty –

   rain-riddled, unsettled by
the drift of its own deep sleepwalking,
   transfigured in journeys through

the tunnels of the bodies
of wormmouths that swallow it, nothing
on earth or in it given

to rest. Like the globe itself
we're all floaters. What we see is one
with where we are and, inspired

by earth's refusal to shake
the dead hand of gravity, we see
ourselves in this buoyancy.

WATER MUSES

Night Music

Head tilted, lips at

the tap trace the water flute's

endless glissando.

Writing Morning

Black teapot pours white

peony tea. Black petals

bloom on the white page.

Copy Editors

Diving shorebirds drop

full stops and commas into

the lake's cursive lines.

Yellow Surfer

Where is the ocean

whose waves this goldfinch in flight

writes above ploughed land?

THE MUSE'S HOME

Come down from your mind's penthouse, that fastness
      deaf to traffic. She can never abide it:
            plate glass glares migraines, bookshelf
dust storms choke her, and from a thin black root
      rises the kitchen's only tree – cold-hearted, flat-crowned,
           leafless. All night, distant pipes promise
                oasis, erasing, erasing.

Come up from your basement apartment.
      How can she sit and write in a bedroom where
           the bed engulfs the room? The rays the small
portholes let in are writhing eels of light,
      scribbled inkblots nest in the sink, the reek
           of sea-swill stings her nose, and plump sofa
                cushions swallow her like ooze.

In search of ground to stand on, air to breathe,
      she walks the torso's paths. Her muscled
           feet find traction on the stepped ribcage.
Beneath the shoulders' ivory arch, she lights
      on earthways, windways, waterways, those streams
           that flow with the silks of sunrise on their backs
           from heart through breath to words.

SHORE HOUSE

On Christopher Pratt's *Porch Light*

It is what you always wished it to be,
a past safer than dreams. Behind that wall
fruit sits unperishing in a bowl, chairs
on their four legs around the table halt
like enchanted ponies, and the mirror's
waters will never be ruffled. You see

none of this, for the wall is windowless
and the overlapped lids of weatherboard
sleep tight. The door's handle may beckon you,
but if you ever gripped that flat white ring,
paint has sealed the door so seamlessly to
sill and frame no crevice would give access

even to a shadow. Nor can you reach
the source of the porch light above the door
though it stares straight at you. Bare frosted bulb,
moon ever full, it follows no orbit
but burns unwavering all night under
the flighty heavens. They now glow pale peach

beside the house, above the sea. Beyond
the painter's grasp, a great red circle will
eclipse his moon and, rolling on, erase
the ruled geometries of fine-pencilled
clapboard slats: blanked with glare, the wall will face
a light that, looked at straight, would burn you blind.

Turn your eye to the sea instead. Mark how
wave-lines near the house mirror the slat-lines
but soon, farther from shore, break free of rules.
Rectangles stretch and pucker in a vine-
like weave that, still farther out, unravels
into random blue and peach satin threads

the horizon shears off. Tattered fabric
of scattered mirrors, the sea reaches in
to you, reminds you how it brought you here
before your walled past. How its white salt runs
through the red of your veins. How you too are,
when most awake, unhoused, your lights unfixed.

THE VINEYARD

How long will it take, when my body is stored in the cask
of the earth, for hands to offer up the bone and muscle
of grasp and fist, and become the undulating, light-filled

fine-veined hands of vine leaves? How long for the backbone's steel shaft
to soften into a questioning whisper, coiling and
resting on whatever support the earth comes up with? How

many tides for thought to purge itself of edge and corner
and be poured into the sea-polished roundness of the grape's
sweet flesh? And how long before blood, shuttling through its tunnels,

becomes this unbound flowering, this blushing face that needs
no mirror because it is one, giving the world the world
dyed into rose heart and rising as the scent of morning.

CORNER BROOK NFLD.

New-found, never-caught,

cod-slippery, the blood's brook

leaps through the heart's grip.

LUCA DELLA ROBBIA'S SINGING GALLERY

Florence, 1431-38

No not just singing   dancing   the little girl lifting
her chubby left foot so high it arches   so high it lifts
the frilled hem of her dress into bubbles of gauze   so

high she must hold her right arm behind   out of sight   her
torso arching over it   balancing on the toes
of her right foot lifting   out over the pedestal's

edge   while the fingers of her palm-up left hand   clench round
and hide   her dancing partner's index finger   so tight
not to keep from falling but to pull   that little girl

out of the flat stone into ripples   and she comes through
her hair streaming   swept back towards the rockface she leaps from
and Luca sees he is not alone in his longing

to free the rivers from the stone   every gliding foot
his chisel strokes   strokes feathers of water in the bed
of marble it wades   every hip-thrust sweeps a cascade

of sheer silk down the facade   the figures liquify
by turns   scroll-singers ambling out of their crystalized
limestone mist   into spume and shimmer   as streams take on

texture by pouring themselves over scree   trumpeters
summoning every curl of their hair into billow
with purls of sound   from water-balloon-plump marble cheeks

hollowing   sluicing through marble tubes   the lutanist
plucking strings   from rock grown sodden   her middle finger
ecstatic   lost in the melt it probes   like a bear's paw

angling into a honey tree   for another lick
a dream seeking   clear solidities of ice   only
for thaw   he would turn   from the hard ware of monuments

to crumbling earth   and bake it   glaze it to hold what is
more buoyant than bone   less fixed than flesh   the vapour trail
of moisture on living skin   he would not live to see

his singing gallery pulled   from its moorings   freed from
the marble-clad Duomo   pried apart panels loosed
on the sidling stream of a wall   stone bubbles   afloat

TO DARWIN IN CHILE, 1835

You will learn to look on every city as Venice,
stone lofted for a while as sun-draped statue before
the tide grinds it to sand. Viewed through the telescopic

glass of geology, mountains collapse to seabeds,
reptiles leave to return as hummingbirds, scallop shells
arise in their brittle white gowns to haunt hilltops banked

over the bones of whales. Yet now, alift with earthquake,
floating on dry land is new to you: "Earth, the emblem
of all that is solid, moves beneath our feet, a crust

over a fluid." You are a skater on wafer-
thin ice, or a ship skidding over a cross-ripple.
The cathedral's portal, tilted seawards, is a prow

of arched oak scudding over bobbing rubble. So much
for founding a church on a rock, you think, when keystones
founder, crack, split, fragment. Even the hand-picked Peter

broke in a single night, cock crow finding him marooned
in a wreckage of denial. Yet if you could call
together all the coloured crystals of the east wall's

stained glass window – most benign form of rock, stone's thinnest
shadow, now shattered to stardust – you would see your life's
and this moment's discoveries lightly prefigured

in the image of another storm-tossed man whose feet
tested earth's rocky sediment and found it seafoam,
walking on water as you do now, as we all do.

GLACIOLOGIST

Think of him as keeper of
an introverted lighthouse.
No blazing wingbeats, no wave-
flocks landing on rock. Muffled
warble from a campstove flame
as it pipes warmth to the wind-
rifled coverts of his tent.

The hours of his days nest in
water, from the kettle's pool
of morning to the noon hole
a calibrated beak makes
probing ice for loss. Evening
sun-thaw from the moulting crag.
Night's shed feathers of crystal.

Glaciologist. Tracking
a glacier. Who will he be
when it's not? Ask who followed
the great auk's dwindling webbed prints.
Ask when his name has melted
into the dark islands left
by the flown notes of songbirds.

NARWHAL

We sleep side-by-side with eternity, and never touch.
         – Sue Sinclair

Or do we touch   and never know   hands grasping a what
lungs spread-eagling their wings   on the bedfellow's warm breath
but embracing only air   eternity conceived

as distant myth   while its womb   is the lap we sleep in
dumbly as unicorns cradle   their ivory lances
in the embroidery of tapestried virgins   those horns

sawn from narwhal bodies left   to redden ice floes   tusks
scraped clean of blood   algae   plankton   all whisper of white-
blanketed seabed hushed   shipped southward   to flute the myth

of otherworldly birth   the dead whorled tube polished   revered
the living narwhal forged   by the human heart's torchlight
to the shape of fear   spike-fanged bloodseeker   sword or spear

or grooved hull-devouring auger   *the most terrible
creature God ever invented*   invented by Verne
while the real narwhal tusk   punctures no kayak   slashes

no flesh   but reaches like a lover's arm   outstretched to
the world   pulses to minute shifts in pressure   opens
closures to the caresses   of the icy saltflow

that threads along its spirals   to whisper tomorrow's
weathers in a sibilant language   syllabled with
yesterday's flood tides   the horn an augur fathoming

currents we hear as white noise   signs on seas or skies we
read as blank slate   no sceptre holding sway   its ivory
set astir in harmony   with an element all

flow   no ground to plant flags   far from the unicorn's dead
pinnacle   the living narwhal's infinite nerve-ends
make love   with the eternities   of air and water

REDBIRD REEF

Valhalla for subway cars   those shining helmeted
ships no longer doomed   to the dark caverns   their windows
purged of glass and city grit   they plunge from the barge through

the seafoam clouds' white smoke   in ashless immolation
released into waterlight   wide door-holes welcoming
the unstoppered draught   after fleeting sips at stations

unwheeled they drift   downward towards landfall   on the sandfloor
where quiet water-breathers   like a sea god's daughters
fill their once clattering halls   with shoeless saraband

deep-centred triple rhythms   of birth and life and death
green veils of sea bass larvae   float in intertidal
water columns   summer flounder eyed like peacock tails

fan out to soften   rivet lines on roofs   blue mussels
sponges   barnacles   sheathe and stud   steel poles with living
jewellery   treasure hoard whose spending   renews itself

gathering eternity from flux   as gills filter
oxygen from water   see how the tautogs hover
free of wind or gravity   on spread wings of their fins

where this red bird   no fire-loving phoenix is reborn
launched clear of metal trammels   into the buoyancy
of those fluttering beings   who have become its heart

LAUNCHED

on the sides   of a no-name tissue box   collage of
photographs   each prised corner by corner   from black matte
catacombs of old albums   or drawn from under dust

of tin-framed glass   or lifted creased   from recesses in
the dry cracked leather of wallets   their privacies now
exposed to fluorescent resurrection   on the shelves

of a thousand supermarkets   tissue-thin instants
peeled   from the layered lives beneath them   an afterlife
on a cardboard scow   they never would have dreamt   their eyes

launching out on a future   all arrowed prow   this pair
robed in windblessed sunlight   the spread hands   of his lapels
held from applause   only by their fresh press   her immense

corsage   a mass of orchids waving back   at the arched
darkness they've just left   or this descendant of Vermeer's
lacemaker   whose baby-skin glazed high forehead   haloes

the smile she casts   at her hand   on the sewing machine's
stainless wheel   or these two little sisters   gripping ice-
cream cones   the licked tops rounded   with their still unmelted

summer   with the oldness of the young   in long ago
monochrome   the ever nowness   of hold-it moments
that outlast waving flowers   survive floral smocking

on outgrown dresses cut   into dustcloths   endure in
a light floating   above wheels buried in rust   beyond
names   like the stand-up ensemble   dad preposterous

in loud plaid shorts   left arm around the bottom of their
toddler   who shoots up plant-like from this base   eyes fixed for
an instant   on eyes nearly touching his   mom smiling

at the camera   her eyes sunspots   brow unshadowed by
the weight   of before or after   undistracted from
the flash   the rocket of their child   forever rising

WATER AND CLAY

1.
A marriage doomed to failure, more deeply
conflicted than he says *tomayto*, she
says *tomahto*, more incompatible
than night owl and rooster. Water all leap

and light, clay buried in its bed; water
spilling secrets, clay's lips sealed. She's thin-skinned,
takes everything in; he's thick as a brick.
Yet, matched against mortals, a winning pair.

As Flood and Slide, both take our breath away,
and the trickle, seep, and swell of water's
more subtle moves baffle us as well as
the heavy going a shovel finds in clay.

2.
Zisha, purple clay (which is what we all
are), shaped to hold warm water (which is what
we all are). Teapot from Yixing. Capped well,
loam quick with liquid shimmer, miracle

coupling of all four elements. Earth, drawn
from the solid depths of Lake Tai's west bank,
was lifted and air-sifted. A kiln's fire
froze the potter's handhold. Fresh spring water

draws flower freshness now from dried tea leaves
beneath the lid's carved plum branch. Arbour where
water and clay within you sip from clay
and water and renew their wedding vows.

STRANGE WONDERS, UNCERTAIN SOURCES

Bottled during travels   stored in the trader's mind   home
in Venice they poured from his lips   a Yangtze broad-backed
as four lagoons   its Grand Canal ribbed by twelve thousand

arched bridges   in one city   whose cavernous human
mouths took in ten thousand pounds of spice   per day   *tell us*
another lie Master Marco   taunted the hometown

urchins   but who could tell   whether rukh birds that snatched up
elephants   and broke them on rocks   or the mountain-scooped
black stone that   once lit   breathed heat all night   merely wafted

through the old merchant's thoughts   or gave purchase like the steppes
he claimed he'd trekked   deserts indented by red-striped
lion paws   and clawed by dwarfed front feet   of serpents with

jaws wide enough to engulf a man   had his wide eyes
taken him in   when he swore the great Khan's flagons tipped
themselves into golden cups   floating in the air at

Xandu   or was it Clemenfu   or Kaiping fu   north-
east of Taidu   or Dadu   which had been Cambalú
the names shimmered and shifted   Zhouzhou to Gouza to

Giogiu to Gingui   so   "it is reasonable to
conclude that when the text says *Gingui* Marco Polo
is referring to *Zhouzhou*"   words as uncertain as

the Yellow River's lower reaches   which pour today
north of Shandong   into a China Sea entered then
at now-landlocked Huaian   his story entering time

not through his lips   but sailing on ink   from the pen of
his Genoese jailmate   Rustichello da Pisa
scribbler of Arthurian romance   whose chivalric

catchwords float in the margins   of his "mangled French" text
none   of its hundred and forty versions   telling quite
the same tale   how could they when the sources   of Polo's

most prized translucent solid   the hard-paste porcelain
blurred and melted   some traced it back to ground-up eggshells
or bones   others to watery chalk   sun-fired   earth-cached

gift from distant ancestors   the word's own parentage
smirched   Italian *porcellano* little pig   out of
porcus Latin slang for female genitals   crossing

with the French *pourcelaine*   cowrie   did Polo for once
at a loss for words   shiver   when he saw threaded shells
spill down the necks of Yunnan's 'idolaters'   or heard

of ancient Shang warriors   found buried with cowries
brimming from their mouths   did the prenatal eye behind
a gaze surfeited with newness   blink back remembrance

of the source of all his wonders   gleaming portal of
maternal orifice   those lips that had poured him out
warm with certain tidings   from the amniotic sea

II

LAMENTS OF THE GORGES

RIVERBANK

Like the scroll itself unsheltered by glass uncontained
by frame the hermitage in Dong Yuan's scroll opens
on water which is the weave of the costumes of time

each thin instant of rain clad only in the brushstroke
from a single bristle dives into the river's wide
basin which nearly encircles the pavilion perched

over it and over the pavilion and its out-
buildings broader strokes of water pelt down like hours
on the uncovered head of the servant who slow-steps

her tray across the courtyard and on the thatch-hooded
head of the man whose feet beat quicker time on the path
that lollops crosswise from mountains where waterfalls hurl

centuries down to the river in stonewhite columns
of foam and where ages before weary ancestors
sought refuge from the storm of time in caves they painted

with eternity deer poised in mid career human
bodies all winged and feathered liftoff court musicians
forever holding flute notes of longing silence posed

as breath which comes and goes how brave of their descendants
to embrace the shifting vapours beyond the cave breath
shared with other mortals whose writing they learned to read

those geese signing with arrowing wing-strokes the coming
of winter to Dong Yuan's valley pines keening and
bowing under the approaching storm the trembling heart-

shaped leaves of paulownia   printing on air the fear
that floated as words   on the moisture of human breath
and clings   to the scroll's time-darkened silk   as sparkling tears

of rain   from the plough the farmer carries   as he leads
in through the gateway   a boy riding that buffalo
half of whose name   and more of whose body   is water.

DISPLACEMENT

Sometimes   her eyes lidded in afternoon sun   the skin
of her hands   butterfly-wing-thin paper   watermarked
by streaming clouds   she opens and closes the conjoined

red paper-cut fish   as if each half   were the slowly
clasping and unclasping wing   of a perched butterfly
the twin carp   having turned gills to lungs   able to sip

and ride air's currents   as they did water's   this kissing
couple   displaced from their river home   as she from hers
on her perch now   dream-catching the river's whisper   in

rapids of traffic   far below the white concrete raft
of their balcony   so some nights   one with the undammed
flow from the apartment's ductwork   her daughter whispers

her from weeping   no cause for tears   with child and grandchild
here   *your cane chair   your own grandmother's Yixing teapot*
your husband's photograph   yet none of them the same   all

ghost-thin to her eyes   wanting the play of water lights
in the old riverside house   their bodies drowned with it
with unripe peaches in the orchard   unpicked beans   with

the river itself   its feathery voice lost under
the reservoir's mountain of water   she remembers
how the end crept up through the last days   no sawtooth waves

ripping the shoreline   no dragon bellowing   only
a slow theft of land   each step the flood took no higher
than the width of a spider leg   you could see nothing

happening but whenever you turned around something
gone the garden narrowed by one row the small green
butterfly barred from its pumpkin blossom by a pane

of sky that separated what was alive from what
had lived and she wondering then and now how could she
live apart from the air that had danced with and married

her breath her unrivered heart withered thin as the red
paper-cut fish whose wings she now flapped · who could take flight
no more than she twice bereaved a riverbank's widow.

PEACHES

How do you revive a drowned river   whose white-threaded
breath has been unstrung   whose flashing swordblades   are no more
than leaden sludge   whose stone armour's chinks lie silt-filled   if

you lived in times before time   you would feed it peaches
fruit ever skinned with the eternal sun   forever
flushed with rising   rife in the gardens of Hsi Wang Mu

goddess who drives the stars   flesh of her fruit so luscious
one bite makes the mouther's flesh immortal   if you lived
in later legendary times   you would turn for help

to peaches   like the fisherman from Wu-ling   who rowed
so far upstream he left the known world behind   landing
on banks of scented trees   and following the petal-

rippled stream   to its source in a low cave   he slipped through
into the sunlit past   a village long preserved from
time's sad spoilage   villagers whose speech was song   whose hopes

were blossom   ancient patterned clothing   freshly woven
and filled with children   but if you lived far inland from
the shore of legend   under a dynasty of dis-

enchantment   which no longer held the miniature
ploughed field   of a peach's furrowed pit   a charm against
deluge   and which viewed the furrowed moon   as no more than

a peach pit in the night sky   its pointed ends rounded
down by sanding rivers of stardust   would you still look
for the ripening peach of a full moon   held captive

in the jade lake   above the river's stilled bones   and would
you dive in to free it   unwilling to give up fruit
you can live on no longer   than you can breathe water?

ANOTHER RIVER

On Edward Burtynsky's photograph, *Feng Jie #5*

Not the roadbed's rubble-banked one   this sweep of "river"
too sluggish to rise on inverted-comma wings   cuts
channels broader than human traffic fills   not that sluice

nor those grey-foamed swells rolling   across the road   over
the heads of a man and his donkey   welling up from
two small fires   the picture's sole bright undoings   silken

shimmers of orange-hooded spirits   that make ash from
the scene's only wood   this river of fouled air gets on
with fire   shares fire's enmity for the water that is

as missing from the picture   as from the moon   ashen
hillside   dust-covered shards of cinder block   dusty man
and donkey   the one non-human form of life   borne on

this river   which supports neither pink Yangtze dolphin
nor finless porpoise   and which has drowned in its torpor
sturgeon and soft-shelled turtle   whose avenging ghosts throng

the river   and possess the bodies   of more deadly
swimmers   endotoxins   benzopyrenes   aerosol
denizens of a bed too wide to bridge   too savage

a tide for any dam to hold   river everywhere
but nowhere in the picture   like a god's messenger
gifted with invisibility   and winged helmet

stronger than hardhats   that will not shield crews spidering
wrecked ramparts in the distance   what chance for tender manes
of donkey or man   as he leads the beast burdenless

and festive in studded red halter   through the river
to sacrifice   do his feet break into a half-run
his face into a smile   in hope of pleasing the god

who lives in the west   whose urgings will deliver him
up   where airborne blades finer than spider legs   sweeping
through the forest of his lungs   will open more rivers

LIUDONG RENKOU

The corpses keep banking up   on this ledge of outcrop
backlit by a moonrise   that blues even the cascades
of Battlehammer blood   spurting from wrist-stumps   for you

must chop off their hands   after you zap them   to harvest
the gold bracelets   each worth fifteen points   it is an art
to swivel the arm   so the spray of blood will not blind

the screen and cost a penalty   but you have to stop
at twenty bodies   before the Fleshmanglers scent you
or Ironfang's impalers show up   game over   still

you are safer on these lower slopes   where explosives
have yet to be invented   you score less   but the worst
you have to fear are the Bloodquest Skullkrushers   nothing

like a Deathtide carpet bombing   wiping out your whole
balance   as in the time   three or four orders before
ASICS   when the sole department was cutting Nikes

on night shift   imagine   coming back to the dorm to
recharge   just as the lights were switching off   on Guangdong
Road's PVC palms   within minutes after going

online   your account plunges to zero   still you can
begin over   you are always 473ZH2YV   see
it's tattooed in code above the wrist   no matter if

roommates leave   or you are switched to another dorm   you
come home to Black Mountain   it will never go under
the waves like old Wushan   trees   caves   the mountain itself

37

floats   at a finger's touch   even should your mobile phone
get stolen   and you lose all your stored friends   that girl on
the bus   who wore her hair like Princess Lunara   you

texted every day   sometimes went online together
she will be there with you   standing on the same stone path
looking up at the same full moon that never changes

WASH

*If you hide your boat in a canyon, and then hide the mountain
in a marsh, you may think the boat is safe and secure.
But something powerful might come in the dead of night,
heave it all onto huge shoulders and carry it away.*
     – Chuang Tzu (365-290 B.C.E.)

Let your boat wash away downstream   on the numbed current
of the drowned river   like a floating   spirit-laden
paper lantern   at the Feast of the Hungry Ghosts   on

to the next world   let the shoulders of its gunwales heft
on planks laid across them   like a bearer's yoke   the full
cargo of your losses   from small offerings you could

touch   a worn toothbrush   an outgrown shoe with one buckle
missing   to the ever unreachable hostages
of the deep   ghost of your face in window glass   among

plum leaves long fallen   on steps of children's forgotten
games   white puffs of child-breath   over frost on a plum branch
and let your boat not capsize   under the greater heft

of streets you will never walk again   in old Wushan
Fengdu   Shibaozhai   under the stones of lost Fengjie's
West Tower   where Du Fu's ghostly finger   still traces

the arc of a setting moon   round white stone   it lowers
itself onto the boat   ripples a silk scarf waving
farewell   but from the vast unmaking of this wash   may

—

making arise   as the heavenly dragon   leaps up each
spring   from the river's jade dungeons   to race through veins of
peach and plum   and blossom as cloud-puffs   whose breath scatters

dead leaves   whose lightning-claws rake down rain   to wash away
winter   and slake the bare earth's thirst   or may creation
take the untouchable shape   of *hsien*   a flowering

of pure spirit   brush-charactered as moonlight broken
free   from its black-wreathed tomb of white stone   a wash of light
through open courtyard gates   or let a fresh world's rivers

and mountains rise   unbrushmarked   from the light and dark wash
of ink   as in the earliest landscape paintings   gift
of artists   whose unsigned lives were boats that sailed away

into the currents of their art   leaving no more trace
than their hands left   on the monochrome's dappled waters
a making   never hostage to the river   never

seeking to cage the dragon   grasp the moonlight   or drink
from streams flowing down a silk scroll   where the no-colour
black   rainbows your washed eye   with all the floating colours

DRAGON

*Spirituality in ancient China was primarily
a matter of dwelling at the deepest levels
of our belonging to dragon's realm.*
      – *Tao Te Ching,* David Hinton, tr.

The latest version   not your standard-issue myth   no
once-upon-a-time chimera   appearing only
to disappear once more   this dragon on the river

abides the now of your presence   and will outlast the
ever of your absence   no mysterious life force
brooding under ice-sheeted pools   breaking from a spring

silkworm's cocoon   this is a solid   joint corporate
creature of East and West   too huge to rise from its lair
too engrossed in its powerful dream   to raise a port-

cullis of plated eyelid   nor must you dream   of tongues
of flame under the breath-clouds   for this dragon's only
fire is water   its reptile blood a flood of white jade

pumped through an iron-hearted turbine   malevolent
even as an egg in the human mind   coercing
valley dwellers to ravage their own lands   drown their crops

pull their houses apart   brick by brick   beam by beam   burn
everything light enough to float   fashion a body
for it   scaled with concrete ridges   impermeable

and bomb-proof   dragon whose sole traditional feature
is deafness   you may scream yourself hoarse   scrape the skin from
your fists beating its flanks   it will not respond except

for shrill piping   can you hear it over the spillway's
roar   from hollows among the half million tons of steel
that are its bones   the dragon's descant to your deep greed

A REVERSAL

On Edward Burtynsky's photographs, *Feng Jie #1 (September 2002)*
and *Feng Jie #2 (November 2002)*

Let's say   as children say   gusts of breath spiriting shape
up from the void   as mist over a sandbox   blossoms
into steamship cloud-puffs   the sandbox itself moving

upon flower-flecked green waves   let's say the two photos
must be read in reverse order   and lo   November's
rubble field in #2   opens as a great void

from which September's grey-ribbed skeletons   will arise
skulls with square eyeholes   arteries of vinyl tubing
all the scattered bones of knuckled rebar   knit and fleshed

with concrete   brought back from the gorge's levelled graveyard
in resurrection   but what child would want to breathe it
into being   city where the wind can only throw

knives sharpened on corners   never nestle up to branch
of pine or wutong   once home to thrush and swallow   dream-
home to phoenixes   city whose only trees are green

mist on far mountains   whose buried streams will never rise
run feathered hands over stones   or lullaby with sky-
larks   how can song   or saying   flower from the vase of

the human throat   so far from the throat-gardens   of lark
or thrush   passerine fliers   gifted with feet that grip
branches of what is green and rooted   that find no hold

on the concrete trunks of September's Feng Jie   let's take
our chances with November   where in only two months
a vine has thrown a green shawl   over the side of what

was once a concrete wall   tenacious riser from no
visible tomb   *ge gen* vine   no stutterer despite
the halting name   thrusts its taproot   through demolition's

grey armour   and under chainmail of shard and dust   finds
lifelines that escape the camera's lens   veins of water
and soil   *ge gen*   herb known by ancient healers to treat

drunkenness   let's say this vine or an offshoot   climbs high
enough to outreach the flood   say it lives long enough
to cure the mad craving   that has choked the gorge's throat.

RECLAMATION: THE CONCERT

On Edward Burtynsky's photograph, *Wan Zhou #2*

Sweet scent-arrows of ginger   released from a cauldron's
curved bow   riding steamcloud currents   up a grey chimney
have survived   the chimney's journey into bricks and dust

as eel-oil-laden winds   borne on the river's back   slip-
ping off   to ride over riverside sedge   have survived
passage from flow   to dry bed   to inundated banks

as eddies of silk-watered sound   unreeling from throats
of thrush and warbler   survive to shimmer over wires
where the birds perched   the air takes everything in   reclaims

as the monochrome   of ancient landscape painting   takes
into its darkroom   rootstock   blossom   cloud-nest and wing
that later eyes may share   in an earthly paradise

of re-creation   infuse ghostly stems with vivid
nectar   thaw the white sky's blue lake   blood the slate traces
of sunset   and rekindle crimson-spangled feathers

———

so these dust-plumed workers   salvaging brick from rubble
pulling bright streams of copper piping   from dry runnels
are the instruments   of air's orchestration   movements

of their bodies   charged   with the city's recollected
rhythms   as all bodies contain and reclaim   earth-heat
star-glow   the music of past lives   so the instrument

in middle foreground   perched on the rooftop we look down
onto   is both a block and tackle   and an *erhu*
its ropes or silk strings   set shuddering with the gorges'

laments   and the wood gripped   by the striped-shirted worker
whose body holds the *S* shape of work's pitch   is pulley
and bamboo hammer   hovering over a *yangqin*

which is also the cap   of a flat-topped pyramid
of bricks   where the kiln's remembered firestorm   survives
in the lightning of struck bronze   while the player squatting

with back turned to us   cradles on an extended leg
a rebar rod that is the knobbed neck   of his *pipa*
singing in duet   with the *tanggu* we can neither

hear nor see   since the crouched back of the worker   who taps
its leather head   hides it from view   but no one can miss
this concerto's solo instrument   three storeys tall

———

warbling apart from the rooftop orchestra   scaling
a ribbed foundation wall that stands   to bridge two levels
of rubble   it is both bamboo trough   and flute longer

than the primal instrument   the god Fu Xi carved from
wutong   a lute   held under a strong current until
wood took the stream's flow into its valleyed heart   and gave   ·

the strings the clarity of water   but this flute flows
clear as the air the valley of its trough   brings to light
workmanlike air   carrying   reclaiming the breath-notes

sung by the last gibbon   in the lost gorges   music
our listening   grants this mute Wan Zhou scene   as our sight
graces the roofless trough   with a flute's complete roundness

ears and eyes inspired to give freely   by all-giving
air   that reclaims poured-out water   and lifts it from earth's
rivers and oceans   imbuing it with the glimmer

of stars   returning it to earth freshened in rounded
rain-notes   ginger-sweet music that breath takes to the heart
where   like the heart of the primal lute   we thirst for song

III

AIRBORNE

———

SOUNDINGS

1. Gorge and Golden Bough

The cavern was profound, wide-mouthed, and huge,
Rough underfoot, defended by dark pool
And gloomy forest. Overhead, flying things
Could never safely take their way, such deathly
Exhalations rose from the black gorge
Into the dome of heaven. (Aeneid VI. 331-6)

waldbühne
forest-stage
poured
concrete amphitheatre
third reich mould

earthbound moon-crater
updated sibyl's cave

a seabed stranded so far
inland the tide incised
only an after image
of moon-phased
retreat

barren furrows ranged
in concentric rings
skeletal ribcage
bone-ridged
shell

you step
down
into death
no pulse not even
waves of wind whose fingers
are more ghostly thin and
aryan pale than
the sea's

here waves of poisoned breath
rose in the thirties
and broke on hitler's private box
sound of shattered
crystal crashing in breakers

sieg heil
trumpeted in
thickest shade
seeped into blackshirted
breathers

if only the golden bough
might shine for us in such a wilderness

——

this evening
leaves of maple
and linden will transfigure
shadow into
green uplift

whisper canopy
of tuning woodwind
throat-music of
the gorge

so bright amid the dark green
the golden leafage rustling in light wind

waves
of tree-breath surging
into song

the tree's fruit with its foliage of gold

2. Glissando

The cavern's hundred mouths all of themselves
Unclosed to let the Sibyl's answers through. (Aeneid VI. 126-7)

The gorge wells up this evening. Percussive wavelets
of sound patter the concrete bowl to the brim.
 Guiding hand clasps stiffened arm: the conductor
leads the blind pianist through the applause and over
   unfamiliar arrangements of footlight and wire.
Ozawa grasps the baton, the Roberts trio's
   hands rise as if to bless bass, drums, keyboard,
and under stars that have outshone torchlit horror,

 brass rows of Philharmoniker horns
tilted like so many gleaming ears, listen.
  Listen for a surge of human breath
reed-teased into music, rushing along
   the clarinet's dark tunnel – so sea water
funnels through a cleft to splay white feathers
   into a silky wingspan stroking the beach –
a spiralling wave of sound. Striking up Gershwin's

 Rhapsody, cool dusk enters the clarinet
warmed, buoyant from its run along the shores
   of blood and bone. It lifts its new-found voice
and takes off, calling up into its slipstream
   a bullfrog boom from the gut of the double bass,
muffled puffs of steam that are the snare drum's
   soul, and distant but clear-ringing pebbles
the piano drops to the heart of its ebony pool.

"Glissando," golden bough traced on the score
in casual flight out of the upper air,
   a wave's light shafted arch branching from one
note-pillar to the next. How but through
  this blueprint for an architecture of air
can the eye make out what the ear takes in –
   dance without steps, gravity-defying
uphill glide, waterless fountaining,

blue bird
      all white wing,
            wing feathered
                 with song.

3. *All With One Accord*

Daedalus, when he fled the realm of Minos,
Dared to entrust himself to stroking wings
And to the air of heaven. (Aeneid VI. 22-4)

Eiderdown, meltdown, or both, like Icarus?
Here twilight blue slips into uniform black,

green leaves bleed to shadow. Poised horns,
woodwinds, and violins are tipped and poured

into one common stream. Features weep
from faces of shades perched on the concrete steps.

But not into nothing. And no plummet – neither
splashy waxwork breakdown nor downdraft flutter

of dove on rushing mighty wind. No ghost
of howl or holiness. Only the honky-tonkish

phantom fingerleaps of ragtime floating over
the keyboard: ghosts of Chico Marx's novelty-

strides in duet with Roberts' living fingers
outrunning the eye's reach like hummingbird wings.

With one accord, white handprints melt into
black hands. Harmonics of a New York Jew's

"Negro music" (a Twenties critic's slur)
catching breath, run through brass corridors

of German French horns, answering the notes
a Japanese conductor's baton writes

on air we all breathe. In this sea of breath,
where does the soul of one breath-river end

and another begin? And what is music but
a boat for soul to sail across unseen waves?

4. Starborn

Neither her face
Nor hue went untransformed . . .
she had felt the god's power breathing near. (Aeneid VI. 77-8, 82)

All waves are unseen by the blind pianist, but on
the black waters of his dark glasses, stars
  of spotlights glitter, and on the calm dark sea

of his piano lid. No *deep world sunk in darkness*
  under the earth. No *Charon foul and terrible*
who *poles his craft* alone. In the twinkling

  runs of his fingers through the high notes' surf
we track the brightest stars, too deep in time
  for lens to find, born ages before our gaze:

our grandest parents, sources of all sun.
  Sparks of their dust, the gods asleep within us,
wait ranged along each cell's spiral strands –

  double helix, waveband of and to
the stars. Spotlit, the sparks awaken and leap
  through notes that ripple Roberts' blue silk shirt,

or through the coruscating silver of
  Ozawa's blaze of hair. His moon-browed eye
winks back at their winking, and they ride

  first on the saxophonist's waves of breath
and then, her instrument at rest, they play
  along the upturned corners of her mouth:

Sibyl, surfacing from her immersion
   with a splash of smile, she is a midnight swimmer
cradled on the blues that *shine for us,*

   as starborn gods rising from our darks
take back the sky. A blossom-shimmer on
   our family tree. The soul-boat's running lights.

SUNTHREADS

From the German of Paul Celan

Sunthreads

over the greyblack voids.

A tree-

high thought catches the lightpitch: there are

still songs to sing beyond

the human.

INCA SKULL

Thy mouth was open but thou couldst not sing.
    – from George Herbert's "Death"

You've got me under your skin, reader – too
scared to let me out. Your fear spreads

a cloth of flesh over my threadbare bone,
paints a pink mouth around the bronzed little

tooth-grove (its tongue-fruit stolen), fills
the empty bin behind my sockets

with enough mind and memory to make
the it of me a he or she. You're no

better than my next of kin, whose hopes
burdened the funeral ark with gear:

slingshot, rope sandals, hammered silver tweezers,
strong *chicha* to knock back, then stomp the pooled

night water awake. But I had sailed through sleep,
beyond one animal dream, spirit scattered

like grain among the multitudes of slither,
creep, and flit. Tweezers will lift raindrops

back into cloud before you, scouring the propped
bone lantern, scrape up a flicker of soul. Better

for us both had enemy axes pummelled the skull plate
to wreckage sticky with scraps – lip tatter, blood-smeared

cheek nugget – not a peekaboo-playing, domed
no-brainer. Nobody's home: stop knocking. Let

the black bird in your eye take wing from that
abandoned nest as mine did. Fly fearless.

Flute song inhuman, beyond a bird's hearing.

LATE AUTUMN REFLECTION ON
THE TREE OUTSIDE MY STUDY WINDOW

The pursuit of light

shaped your bones. Come leaf-fall, may

mine be as comely.

HEAVENLY UPNESS

Upness and downness . . . are . . . pure sensation.
                                    – William James

And upness is the purest. At puberty,
in the bath, thoughts of some earthly paradise

would turn the floater lolling in the foliage
below my waist into a rising arrow,

divining rod pointing towards the unearthly
waters of heaven.

                        Another upwardly

mobile trickster sprang from Kwakiutl legend:
Mink, taunted by his playmates as a bastard,

but sure his own red marrow proved him child and
heir to the sun, shot arrows at earth's roof. Each

one took root in the nock of the one before,
a ladder he climbed to his father's house.

                                    You

know in your bones the house of the sun is your
real home. What but this thought-shaft, shot from the brain,

lifted our trickster elders on their hind legs
to walk from the monkey house? Arrow ladder,

carved from the wood of heaven-bent trees and fledged
with plumes from birds aloft on pure rising

                                    song.

ARISE AND STAY

Heaven lies about us in our infancy
until we learn the hallowed lie about it
that locks it up: cloud palace in the sky
waiting for the gold key, death, to open it.

Open your eyes: heaven rises in the house
of here and now, as surely as dawn warblers
breathe out song clouds against the country darkness
or goldenrod fountains from city rubble.

Look – even the iron nails are so intent
on heaven they've thrust into the ceiling beam
over their heads, leaving in the wood's slow stream
a ripple halo where each one ascended.

As your heart's lips know only the song of blood,
your walls are heaven's, this sun-spill is its gold.

PLANETARY EVOLUTION

The nostrils of his four horses were torches.
The hooves struck sparks on heaven's thinnest air.
Only Apollo could hold the white-hot reins.
Gold chariot, arrowing flame through the night walls.

Totalled in the wreck of mythology,
its chassis picked clean by time, his chariot's
only a spokeless yellow wheel that rolls
from east to west over the garage next door.

Which stays put while its roof-peak aims a long
shadow arrow across cool morning grass
and down the warmed concrete driveway of afternoons.
Stable shape above the tides of light

rippling the lawn's green bay. Anchored ark,
all the more ark at both ends where the wrestle
of rain-drench and sun-parch have wrenched clapboard planks
into the upturns of a bow and stern.

Until this morning, when our neighbour rested
the top of a round picnic table against it
and blundered into legend and evolution.
The slatted, wheel-shaped top's diagonal lean

steeps it in motion, as the upward thrust of planks
at front and back lift the garage from ark

to winged chariot, arrowing over earth
forever spinning eastwards underneath.

DIMINUENDO ON THE THEME OF WHETHER
SHAKESPEARE'S MONUMENT BEARS
HIS TRUE LIKENESS

Brood-pouch of brain, nest of mouth, tongue-
branch that quivered when his words
flew off: rain-swept with fall's
paper birds out of
air, into earth
blind to wing,
deaf to
song.

No hope from stone, left breathless by
its weight, too dense to rise to
a tune. Even paper
covers rock. Water
chisels it a-
way, unmon-
uments
it.

What fine chisel, he wrote, *could . . . cut
breath?* Asking the question sculpts
the answer, incisor
flicking lip and tongue
to carve fluted
words on lung-
quarried
air.

Not stone, but birdcall. Read his word
excitement. It quivers, lifts
from the lines' black branches,
finds its song in the
clear blue of your
mind and sweeps
through your
lips.

BLUEGRASS

starts with   mouth-to-mouth inspiration   from the beige-lipped
perfect   O   of a Martin D-28 guitar
where soul on rebound   from plucked brass   swims up through sound waves

and waits humming   behind a copse of hair   at the mouth
of an ear-cave   for the high lonesome sound   another
soul breaks into   when it breaks as breath   out of its white

ribbed chest-cave   slips on a jumpsuit of song   from the red
walls of the singer's mouth   rides the trilled riptide outwards
and partners its soulmate   to sashay down the vaulted

canal   career off tautened eardrum   toggle hammer
on anvil   and tickle the coiled-up cochlea   but
the true beginnings of bluegrass   echoed through ancient

rock caves whose high roofs   hummed duets with stone-age singers
enchanted by warm overtones   the icy limestone
draped around their solitary voices   longing to

prolong the partnership   between what lasts   and what runs
out of breath   seeking to carry   harmony with them
as a body   out of the cave   finally lighting

on wood   carved into a heart shape   too full of singing
to taper to a point   curved like a woman gravid
with new music   soundboard braced by rosewood ribs   slim neck

drawing out voice cords   like drops of water drawn into
needles   wept from cave roofs   brimming with human sorrow
yet plucking joy   from hearing unhuman wood echo

their song in its own bright voice   even on starless nights
as if they had come   at the farthest reach of a cave's
dark passage   into a place of green skies   and blue grass

TWO OLD MEN ARE FOUR BIRDS

Because each of us is always two birds the first one
born into skin's smooth pouch but fledged through living wet winds
driving quills into creases scored by every sunrise

the second one slowly gestating through a lifetime's
nights when the body lies down and draws itself into
an egg dreaming the incarnation it will take on

after its last moult so those bodies buffeted to mottled
sparrows dream on their litters of rubbish of hatching
into the silk-lined nest and wide skies of the goldfinch

and creaky bottom-heavy mourning doves of trading
the elaborate origami of their plumage
in for the flame-edged scissors of a barn swallow's wings

so Studs Terkel at age ninety-five prepares to yield
the dour accoutrements of crow a stiff cape blackened
by omnivorous acts of sympathy that took in

the sooty fumings of factory workers rendered
roadkill in hard times a caa-caa-call the species sign
of true shit-disturbers soon shucked off already red

jackets his breast and his voice's scratchy old record
will break into brook water carolling *skip skip skip*
free free free to stones it glides over as a new song

flies from his cardinal heart velveting the same glade
a downy woodpecker's flak will no longer rifle
when Bernard Adler gives up the Singer that has stitched

together the frayed ends   of his eighty-seven years
from the camps   where he sewed Nazi uniforms   ("if not
a tailor   no surviving")   to his Riverdale perch

above the Hudson   at the Hebrew Home   woodpecker
shuttle bobbing as he guides the cloth   woodpecker head
nodding more slowly   as the Torah mends him   if your

ear can pierce   the stillness that will follow   at sunset
you will catch threads of song   a swift's wings   too high for sight
gather the golden folds of day   pleat them seamlessly

THE ANGELS OF WINTER

It must be the urgency   the sincerity of
her prayer   that summons them   to dance above the cardboard
square she lives and sleeps on   over the subway grating

not kinship   for her shoulder-length hair hangs tangled   black
scored with grey   not the gold cascade   of painted angels
her flannel shirt and track pants   worlds from red velvet robes

shouldering harps   mutant butterflies whose supersized
pinions   glued on by a brush   can never hover like
these real angels who   though six-winged   surf on a whisper

her whisper that they come   as blossoms   fill leaf-absence
on the cold bare arms of trees   brim ice-rimmed trash barrels
with splays of floppy stemless paperwhites   and they come

by the millions at her call   not because she calls them
but from love   to caress the grime on sidewalks   embrace
battered refuse   dress the asphalt's wounds   with their kisses

the sparkling ferns of their wings   whose colour is a clear
lightbringing shimmer   of microscopic lips hymning
the six-syllabled mantras of our needs   in purest

silence   melting not immortal   each flickering span
more brief than moth-flutter   a flight all fall   hurtled through
scourging ice clouds   facets hacked   pockmarked like the red cheeks

some land on   others leaping to ruin on her tongue
and some in mid-air thawing to air   breathed in   will soothe
the leafless branches   in the forest of her lungs   in

sisterhood   for who is more homeless   than snowflakes here
every human exhalation rising   like a prayer
that answers itself   as the spent breath   fills with angels

OZ: A TRIBUTE TO GERDA TARO

No going back to Kansas for this girl   Auntie Em
and the other aunts and uncles   already being
rounded up   and ushered into boxcars   no lion

or tin man to pull them out   no pail of tears to quench
flames sending scarecrows   up the chimneys   her filming done
two years before the movie shoot begins   her gravestone

will be carved by Giacometti   levelled by Nazis
and replaced with concrete   but she cares no more for stone
than for going back   to being Gerta Pohorylle

Polish typist   swept from Leipzig by the swastika's
twister   her yellow brick road   leading to Paris where
in place of ruby slippers   she clicks the shutter of

a Rollei   and learns to soar   beyond her typewriter's
clattering wings   the feather stroke of the aperture
outflying flight   lifting her into a self-made star

flash-lit like Garbo   shimmering with the magic art
of Tarō Okamoto   mere dazzle until Spain
focuses her heart   on other refugees   bodies

hunkered in shelters and dugouts   spread unlullabied
on marble slabs   wide-open eyes   demanding she look
not at but through their lenses   over the rainbows of

their irises   above the chimney tops of Europe
to the pure rising   they dare to dream   and her snapshots
find it   not in the skies   but in their living bodies

amid the rubble of bombed Córdoba   children turn
a fallen beam into a see-saw   in defiance
of gravity and blackshirts   a blind musician floats

on the carpet   of his concertina's unfolding
notes   and two running soldiers lift into symmetry
a pas de deux   on the monochrome   where you'll find them

THE MONARCH BUTTERFLY MIGRATION, 1943

For Homero Aridjis, poet and environmentalist

That year   after sun-aproned earth   brought forth her paler
ochre yield of chickpea and maize   blue air broke into
a blossoming of flame   more millions of orange petals

than you or your brothers had ever seen   floating free
of any bough   or invisibly branching   bloom from
a water-clear tree   wider than the mountain   higher

than its fir-crowned summit   monarchs in silk robes rippled
along village streets   lapped into open casements   spilled
down from pink stucco walls   over the cold white skin of

crosses where votive candles   blinked and wept   to welcome
home these souls of the village dead   alighting   folding
their wings in momentary prayer   before taking up

winter quarters in the palace of firs   pillars their
enamelled wings mosaiced   in return for wood warmth
you breathed on morning walks   too young at three to take in

how these hangers-on   could so outnumber all the souls
one town might lose   but wise enough even then to sense
a miracle (your word)   in their coming   how could your

peaceful hills   dream of their flying   from firebombed cities
in Europe   know of the flame tornados that wrenched trees
from earth   gables and roofs from houses   human spirits

from the blackened chrysalids   of incinerated
children   breath-looted elders   bodies shrivelled too small
for hearts seeking the freedom to fly   why would they not

choose this metamorphosis of flame   when cathedrals
were shattering this soft floating stained glass blazoned like
tropical fruit   segments of sun-sweetened fire   contained

by the thinnest black bands   unfraught with memory larval
vestiges of crawl and clutch   sloughed off in an old world
whose wars   your namesake darkly sang o singer facing

down a shrieking ground assault where metal fangs gnaw at
the cross-tipped steeples of fir   that have sanctuaried
these fragile monarchs   of the unrelenting spirit

o lover of mountain streams that echo   the soft rain
of rallying wings   sing the rhythms you share with them
that heart and butterfly may lift   and find their way home.

THE KITE FLYER, NOTTAWASAGA BAY

For John Sanders, hidden 1943-1945

If he starts   by making a stick person   attaching
the outstretched arms   of the shorter piece of dowelling
to the spine   of the longer   it is because he needs

to send this childish wooden replica   of the child
he was then   up to the heavens   to meet the first words
he read aloud   where they still float   and tell them again

to the spirit of his father   floating there   because
when the child spoke them   in Leiden   the father was out
of hearing   in Amsterdam   behind a revolving

closet door   and as he tucks   the sail material
lovingly over the frame   his hands will remember
the hands of a loving stranger   smoothing the blanket

he hugged through unheated nights   his head buried under
the pillow   his ears kept from hearing   not by the pillow
but by his minder's closed lips   of other children

bedded on wet leaves   deer in the forest   on the run
from arm-banded hunters   he too will run   not in flight
but for it   to launch the finished kite   a man pursued

by grandchildren   no place to hide them on this shoreline
no need   feet splashing one lake   eyes fixed on another
where the liberated soul   trails a wake of ribbons

CURIOUS GEORGE TAKES FLIGHT, 12 JUNE 1940

That red balloon on a string   is really his heart   how
else will it carry him so far   how else will it lift
Margret and Hans with him   this morning they lower him

into a basket   like the infant Moses   swaddled
in overcoats   to float above their bike wheels   sidling
through rushes of cars   taxis   horse-drawn wagons   people-

stocked pickups   along cobbled *allées*   where days from now
Nazi tanks will rattle   while Hans and Margret pedal
George can only sit   holding his balloon   in a tree

on the cover drawing   of their still-unpublished book
infant   to be born abroad   image of his parents
those buoyant colours   from mother's Bauhaus lore   handed

down   and from father's Hamburg zoo sketchings   those trapeze
leaps   tonight they'll sleep on a barn floor   wake under stars
not needed   to find their way through lost Europe   for George

will lead them from his cover page   unborn child seeing
times unborn   how else could he have guided Hans's brush
to make his bony perch   prefigure in leaflessness

tree skeletons   of a firebombed Hamburg zoo   how else
would the Reys' drawings have imaged   in his sea voyage
to the "big city"   theirs   four months from now   holding hands

at the ship's rail   as their gaze climbs   with primate sureness
the extended arm of Liberty   so George midway
through the manuscript   stands at a prow   his arms aping

the freedom   of a seagull's extended wings   this child
the parent   when Margret holds a monkey pose   or Hans
mimics treetop chatter while he draws it   George guides them

from flaming cities   through forests of pure animal
instinct   remote from possession   invulnerable
to occupation   leads them into his harmony

so deeply they draw the notes   in their children's songbook
as hearts strung on the bridge of Avignon   gives their hearts
the courage to redraft   a yellow star of reproach

into wearable sun   the yellow hat of rescue
teaches them   though they lack the thumb on his monkey foot
how to fly by gripping that string   tightly as he does.

A CHINESE RIVER IN BROOKLYN

For Amy K. Epstein, its source

Like all New Yorkers   although at a remove
from lower Manhattan   she would shiver whenever
a banking plane's engines mimicked that targeted plunge

or sun-glare on the river mirrored the mirrored flames
or a burst of black smoke from some hidden chimney smudged
across white facades   so she will pardon my first sight

for having read holocaust behind the orange glow
and drifting haze of this landscape painting   which reflects
in its hush of white silk no disaster   but our shared

love for a thousand-year-old scroll by Dong Yuan   his
river valley and banked mountains   a beckoning depth
behind her watery strokes   his monochrome quickened

by her bright palette into this sunrise   where we perch
on the right foreground's rocky promontory   giddy
at the miles of air dangling from its two trees   bleary

with morning mist   down to the river below and out
to the muscled backs of distance-dwarfed mountain ranges
our giddiness witness to one of the miracles

of art   as an eleven inch square of silk   draws us
out of narrow hemmed lives   into a thousand-year-wide
vista   lit by a still older sun's   life-giving fire

AIRBORNE

Bone flute   brittle little cave   cached within a stone cave
long after the flesh and feathers   of the mute swan   whose
wing bone it was   turned dust   dispersed   grew one with the air

bone flute   stone-age act of atonement   for turning flight
and beauty into food   each carved notch   re-enacting
an arrow's interrogation   of a white flank   each

bone flute   a gift of breath   essence of the carver's life
filling and taking flight   from the bleached contours   that had
lifted the swan on fledged wings   more supple than any

bone flute   yet never thrilled with song   until human breath
waking   gave voice and lilt to an upsurge   dormant in
the marrow   larynx turned syrinx   in the throat of your

bone flute   o piper   lightening your cave's endless night
knowing a hollow wing bone   allowed broad-shouldered swans
to float free from earth's pull   did your night vision sweep the

bone flute's shrouded canyon   and see in its emptiness
the bed for an underground spring   of sound   a spirit-
passage flowing from your mouth   through the cave's   or did this

bone flute appear no riverbed   but a wing once more
to ride to paradise   through walls of stone and flesh   nest
in a grove within the song   close your lips   on the sweet

bone fruit.

NOTES

"Luca della Robbia's Singing Gallery": Della Robbia, later known
for glazed terracotta sculpture, first achieved fame for the marble
organ gallery (*Cantoria*) he carved for the Duomo. Its ten bas-relief
panels bring Psalm 150 to life by depicting girls, boys, and putti
singing in harmony, playing the psalm's instruments of praise, and
dancing. Replaced by a Baroque pulpit in 1688, the detached panels
have hung since 1889 in the Museo dell'Opera del Duomo beneath a
reconstruction of the original gallery.

"To Darwin in Chile, 1835": As a young naturalist, long before his
ideas on evolution developed, Charles Darwin witnessed a massive
earthquake that left the Chilean city of Concepción and its cathedral
in ruins. The passage in quotation marks is from his diary account.

"Redbird Reef": Redbird Reef is an artificial reef off the coast of
Delaware, made from scrapped subway cars and now teeming with
marine life.

"Strange Wonders, Uncertain Sources": Passages in double quotes are
taken from Peter Harris's editorial comments in *The Travels of Marco
Polo, the Venetian* and from Colin Thubron's introduction to it (New
York: Alfred A. Knopf, 2008).

Laments of the Gorges: 2009 marked the completion of the
Three Gorges Dam at the heart of the Yangtze River. During its
construction 13 cities, 140 towns, and 1350 villages were submerged,
and 1.2 million people were displaced. Countless historical and
cultural sites disappeared from an area central to over a thousand
years of landscape painting and poetry – an art that held the
possibility of a relationship between humanity and nature based on
reciprocity rather than exploitation. My sequence explores some of
that heritage and the human and environmental concerns associated
with the Gorges, and takes its title from Meng Chiao's ninth-
century sequence about them. My syllabic and stanzaic form pays
homage to the fixed characters of Chinese poetry, while the absence

of conventional punctuation attempts to realize something like the open, juxtapositional syntax of that poetry. These formal strategies have been enlisted, here and elsewhere in this collection, with the aim of involving the reader as active participant rather than passive spectator, often in the hope of evoking a fuller participation not just in the poems but in the issues they raise.

"Riverbank": The painter Dong Yuan was active from the 930s to the 960s. *Riverbank*, his most famous scroll, inaugurated a central tradition in Chinese landscape painting. It currently hangs in New York's Metropolitan Museum of Art.

"Peaches": The goddess Hsi Wang Mu lived in a palace at Jasper Lake in the mythical Kun-lun Mountains. Magic peaches of immortality grew in her garden. In "Peach Blossom Spring," the poet T'ao Ch'ien (365-427) tells the story of a Wu-ling fisherman who happens on a village caught in a time warp, somewhat like Brigadoon. The later poet Li Bai (701-762) is said to have drowned while trying to embrace the moon's image in a river.

"*Liudong Renkou*": The title means "floating population" and is a disparaging popular term for China's estimated 130 million migrant workers. Many of them are so perpetually uprooted that the only constants in their lives are the video games which absorb the little free time they have.

"Another River": Burtynsky's photograph is reproduced in *Before the Flood* (Toronto: Mira Godard Gallery, 2003), along with those referred to in "A Reversal" and "Reclamation: The Concert." The Yangtze dolphin, finless porpoise, white sturgeon, and soft-shelled turtle are all virtually extinct as a result of environmental mismanagement.

"Wash": The Feast of the Hungry Ghosts is a traditional holiday celebrated on the fifteenth day of the seventh month. In the Gorges area, floating lanterns were lit to direct the souls of the drowned to the afterworld. Wushan, Fengdu, Shibaozhai, and Fengjie have all been submerged in the dam construction. The poet Du Fu (712-770) wrote some of his finest work in the West Tower of Fengjie. *Hsien*, usually translated as "idleness," implies in Buddhist contexts a state of receptivity to spiritual illumination.

"Soundings": This sequence celebrates a 2003 Berlin Waldbühne performance of Gershwin's *Rhapsody in Blue* by the Marcus Roberts Trio and the Berlin Philharmonic conducted by Seiji Ozawa. The poem associates the Waldbühne, a gorge-situated amphitheatre where Nazi leaders attended light opera in the 1930s, with the gorge where Virgil's Aeneas heard the Sibyl's dark prophecies. The title of section 3 comes from another text of prophecy, the description of Pentecost in Acts 2.1-6. All italicized phrases are from Robert Fitzgerald's translation of the *Aeneid*.

"Two Old Men Are Four Birds": The two old men are Studs Terkel, activist, broadcaster, and historian of working-class America, and Bernard Adler, tailor and Holocaust survivor.

"Oz: A Tribute to Gerda Taro": Gerda Taro was the first woman photojournalist, born Gerta Pohorylle in Germany in 1910 and killed in 1937 while covering the Spanish Civil War. She constructed her pseudonym to combine the glamour of Greta Garbo with the artistic credo of the painter and sculptor Tarō Okamoto, who proclaimed that "art is magic" and that art should recognize no boundaries.

"The Monarch Butterfly Migration, 1943": Homero Aridjis grew up in the 1940s in the Mexican village of Contepec, Michoacán, where millions of monarch butterflies would winter each year. For accounts of the 1943 firebombing of Hamburg, see W. G. Sebald, *On the Natural History of Destruction*, Hans Erich Nossack,

The End: Hamburg, 1943, and Jörg Friedrich, *The Fire: the Bombing of Germany, 1940-1945*.

"Curious George Takes Flight, 12 June 1940": Margret and Hans Rey, creators of the Curious George children's books, grew up in Hamburg in the early 1900s. Their own curiosity sent them travelling first to Brazil and then to Paris in the 1930s. Two days before the Nazi invasion they fled the city on bicycles, carrying the manuscript of the first Curious George book and making their way by train and ship through Spain and Portugal, back to Brazil, and finally to New York where the book was published.

"A Chinese River in Brooklyn": Amy K. Epstein's silk painting, *River and Mountains*, is reproduced as the frontispiece of this book, and a detail from it is reproduced on the cover.

ACKNOWLEDGEMENTS

Earlier versions of some of these poems, sometimes with different titles, appeared in *Canadian Literature, The Fiddlehead*, the *Literary Review of Canada, The Malahat Review, Our Times, Rhythm, Saranac Review, Vallum, The Walrus, The Windsor Review*, and in *Poetry as Liturgy*, ed. Margo Swiss (St. Thomas Press, 2007) and the chapbook *Laments of the Gorges* (Alfred Gustav Press, 2011). Thanks to all the editors, and especially to Jared Bland, Ross Leckie, Bruce Meyer, Moira MacDougall, and David Zieroth, for their continuing encouragement. Thanks also to the judges in annual competitions for the recognition given to "The Vineyard" by *The Fiddlehead* and to "Displacement" by *Vallum*. I am also happy to thank the Jackman Humanities Institute for the generous Research Fellowship that freed me from teaching duties and supported my reading and writing in 2010.

This book has accumulated more debts than usual in its evolution, as I have picked the brains and drawn on the expertise of friends and acquaintances near and far. For insights about Chinese poetry, music, and landscape, I have benefited greatly from delightful conversations and correspondence with Zhou Yan, translator, poet, art historian, and treasured friend. In that area, I have also learned much from the writings of Maxwell K. Hearn of the Metropolitan Museum of Art, and from the writings and translations of David Hinton, whose versions of Chuang Tzu and Lao Tzu I have quoted from in this book, and whose translation of Meng Chiao brought to life the landscape of the ancient Gorges. Edward Burtynsky's photographs of the Gorges Dam upheavals provided a constantly sobering and suggestive counterpoint to the classical art associated with the region. Closer to home, Kelley Aitken encouraged me to write on Christopher Pratt, and generously produced a fine pastel portrait of *Porch Light* for me when the Art Gallery of Ontario took it off display. I am also indebted to Wayne Clifford for sharing both my enthusiasm for bluegrass and his luthier's knowledge of wood.

Once again, my writing has been privileged to receive the incomparable editorial care of Don McKay. His vision of the whole collection and his kind attention – characteristically both painstaking and stimulating – to individual poems have made this a stronger book, and his friendship and support during its gestation have been invaluable.

Once again, too, members of the Vic writing group have been a steady source of enlightened criticism; this time, I owe particularly warm thanks to Allan Briesmaster, Maureen Hynes, Ruth Roach Pierson, and Leif Vaage. At Brick Books, I'm indebted to Kitty Lewis's infectious and tireless enthusiasm for poetry, to Cheryl Dipede's inspired design ideas, and to Alayna Munce's astonishing eye for detail – both meticulous and generous. My most profound debt is as always to my wife Julie, who has helped to shape the course of every line of every poem with her unstinting devotion to the writing and to its lucky writer.

JOHN REIBETANZ was born in New York City, grew up in the eastern United States and Canada, and put himself through university by working at numerous unpoetic jobs; he is probably the only member of the League of Canadian Poets to have belonged to the Amalgamated Meat Cutters union. Author of seven previous collections of poetry, he has been shortlisted for the national ReLit Award for Poetry and won first prize in the international Petra Kenney Poetry Competition. He lives in Toronto and teaches English and creative writing at Victoria College, where he received the first Victoria University Teaching Award.